STEP-BY-STEP

50 Quick & Healthy Vegetarian Dishes

STEP-BY-STEP

50 Quick & Healthy
Vegetarian Dishes

Annie Nichols

Photographs by James Duncan

SMITHMARK

This edition published in 1994 by
SMITHMARK Publishers Inc.
16 East 32nd Street
New York
NY 10016

SMITHMARK books are available for bulk purchase for sales
promotion and for premium use. For details write or call
the manager of special sales, SMITHMARK Publishers Inc.
16 East 32nd Street, New York, 10016; (212) 532–6600

ISBN 0-8317-7847-4

Produced by Anness Publishing Limited
1 Boundary Row
London SE1 8HP

Editorial Director: Joanna Lorenz
Series Editor: Lindsay Porter
Designer: Peter Laws
Jacket Designer: Peter Butler
Photographer: James Duncan
Stylist: Madeleine Brehaut

Printed and bound in Italy by Graphicom S.r.l., Vincenza

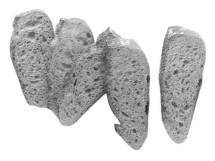

CONTENTS

INTRODUCTION

Vegetarianism is gaining an increasingly favorable image, and has come a long way from the heavy 'brown' food that was so prevalent over 20 years ago. These days the pressure is on to provide fresh, light, innovative ideas for the ever-increasing number of vegetarians. With the proliferation of new and exotic ingredients now available, exciting and imaginative dishes can be made with ease, drawing on a host of wonderful fresh produce and flavors.

A healthy vegetarian diet is easier to achieve than you might think. It is now generally accepted that about 50–70 percent of our diet should be made up of foods rich in the complex carbohydrates that are found in cereals, grains, fruits and vegetables. These ingredients are naturally abundant in a well-balanced vegetarian diet and also have the advantage of being naturally low in fat. With the addition of nuts and beans, they will provide sufficient protein to meet the body's requirements. If you include dairy foods in your vegetarian diet, moderate the consumption of those high in fat, and choose skim or low-fat milk, low-fat yogurt and low- or medium-fat cheeses. Cheeses with a higher fat content, such as Parmesan, may be used in small amounts – as they are strong in flavor a little goes a long way. Control your use of oils, and choose unsaturated types such as olive, sunflower, corn or peanut. Using a non-stick frying pan will also help reduce the amount of fat used in cooking.

By combining a variety of different foods, a well-planned vegetarian diet will provide all the nutrients needed to maintain good health. This book contains dishes from all around the world, with something to suit every taste and occasion, proving that vegetarian food is both healthy, and anything but boring.

Fresh Fruit and Vegetables

Thanks to the amazing range of fresh produce now available, the vegetarian repertoire has expanded enormously. Filled with complex carbohydrates, protein, vitamins and minerals, fresh fruit and vegetables are essential to a healthy vegetarian diet.

Alfalfa sprouts
These crisp, sprouting seeds with a delicious nutty flavor are highly nutritious and rich in protein, fiber, vitamins and minerals.

Baby corn
These young corn are most delicious when lightly cooked, so are especially suitable for stir-fries.

Broad beans
The plump inner bean is delicious when lightly steamed, and makes a good accompaniment to richly flavored foods.

Celeriac
This underrated vegetable has a delicious, sweet, celery-like flavor.

Chillies
There are hundreds of varieties of these hot relatives of the capsicum family. They should be treated with caution. When preparing chillies take special care to avoid rubbing your eyes or face as their juices can irritate the skin.

Fennel
A crisp, delicious, sweet aniseed-flavored vegetable, which can be eaten raw, finely sliced, or cooked. Add a little to vegetable stock for an unusual extra flavoring.

Limes
Fresh and sharp with an intense sour flavor.

Okra
Okra lends a creamy, silky consistency to vegetable dishes.

Patty pan squash
These lovely, scallop-edged baby squash have a similar flavor to zucchini.

Peas
Sweet, tender peas, popped fresh from the pod are unbeatable. Make the most of them when in season.

Pumpkins
There are many different varieties of these members of the gourd family. A thick tough skin belies the fragrant, pale or bright orange flesh within.

Red onions
Mild and sweeter than most onions, their purple flesh makes a pretty addition to any vegetable dish.

Sweet potatoes
The skin of these tubers can be pinkish or brown and the flesh varies from creamy white to yellow or pale orange. Despite its name, this vegetable is not related to the everyday potato. The sweet potato usually has an elongated shape, although some round varieties are available.

Tomatoes
Recent demand for full-flavored tomatoes means that many varieties now abound, from the sweet little cherry tomatoes, to the plump Italian plum and the large beefsteak tomatoes.

Turnips
Sweet, nutty-flavored turnips range from the walnut-sized baby roots (that are often sold still attached to their green tops) to large mature turnips.

fennel

okra

turnips

pumpkin

celeriac

tomatoes

chillies

broad beans

plum tomatoes

cherry tomatoes

sweet potatoes

peas

alfalfa sprouts

red onions

putty pan squash

limes

baby corn

Pasta, Beans and Grains

Pasta, pulses and grains all belong to the important complex carbohydrate group. Most are low in fat and contain plenty of vitamins, minerals and dietary fibre.

Adzuki beans
A small, reddish brown, shiny bean with a unique strong nutty, sweet flavor.

Arborio rice
One of the best and most commonly available rices to use for risotto.

Basmati rice and brown basmati rice
Harvested from the foothills of the Himalayas with a very distinctive, fragrant aroma.

Black-eyed beans
Sometimes referred to as black-eyed peas, these small beans with a black spot have a savory flavor and succulent texture.

Bulgur wheat
A whole wheat grain that is steamed-dried and cracked so it only needs brief soaking before use.

Campanelle
A pretty frilled, twisted pasta tube.

Cannellini beans
These look like small white kidney beans and belong to the same family. They have a soft texture when cooked.

Capellini
Known as angel-hair pasta, this is a very fine variety.

Chick-peas
These pale golden-brown, hard peas look rather like small dry hazelnuts. They have a rich nutty flavor.

Couscous
Made from coarse semolina, this lovely soft grain is now produced to need only a brief moistening before use.

Egg noodles
The most common of all oriental noodles, they take only minutes to cook.

Flageolet beans
Pale green, long and slim, these are navy beans removed from the pod while young. They have a tender texture when cooked.

Green lentils
This superior lentil is prized for its flavor and texture.

Long-grain rice and brown long-grain rice
Long, translucent grains are valued for their nutty flavor.

Navy or white beans
These oval cream beans are commonly seen as canned baked beans.

Oatmeal
Sliced whole oat grain which is graded from pinhead (the coarsest) to medium and fine (medium is shown here). A good source of calcium, potassium and iron.

Pasta bows
The Italian name for this is *farfalle* or 'butterfly', because of its shape.

Penne
Short, tubular pasta shapes, also known as quills.

Polenta
Fine yellow cornmeal, used to make a soft porridge.

Soup pasta
This tiny pasta comes in many different shapes.

Spaghetti
The most popular pasta, it has long, thin strands.

Tagliatelle
Flat, long ribbon noodles. The green version is flavored with spinach.

Wild rice
Not a true rice but the seed of an aquatic grass. The brown, long grains open when cooked.

spaghetti

egg noodles

capellini

campanelle

tagliatelle

soup pasta

pasta bows

penne

arborio rice

wild rice

basmati rice

long-grain rice

brown long-grain rice

brown basmatic rice

polenta

bulgur wheat

oatmeal

green lentils

flageolet beans

cannellini beans

couscous

adzuki beans

black-eyed beans

navy beans

chick-peas

The Vegetarian Kitchen Cupboard

Although not strictly essential, the ingredients listed here will greatly enhance any vegetarian dish, and are convenient to have on hand when preparing food at the last minute.

Balsamic vinegar
A deliciously smooth, rich, sweet-and-sour flavored vinegar made in Modena in northern Italy.

Hazelnut oil
A richly flavored nutty oil. Just a few drops will lift the flavor of a plain salad.

Olive oil
This is high in mono-unsaturated fats and vitamin A. It ranges from the refined pale yellow variety to the rich herbaceous extra-virgin.

Raspberry vinegar
A sweet, light vinegar with the slight tang of raspberries.

Sesame oil
This delicious, rich oil is often used in oriental cuisine as a flavoring rather than as a cooking oil.

Sunflower oil
A mild polyunsaturated oil that is useful for all types of cooking.

Sun-dried tomatoes
A preserved tomato which can be bought either in bags or steeped in olive oil in jars.

Tahini
A paste made from ground sesame seeds, it is widely used in Middle Eastern cooking.

Walnut oil
High in polyunsaturates, this is a delicious nutty oil.

Herbs

Herbs can be used to enliven many dishes with aroma, flavor and color. Use fresh herbs whenever possible.

dill

rosemary

marjoram

oregano

sage

bay leaf

Basil
This herb has a rich, peppery, spicy smell and flavor, and has a perfect affinity with tomatoes.

Bay leaf
These glossy, dark green leaves are an essential ingredient of the classic *bouquet garni*.

Chervil
A delicate, feathery herb similar to parsley with a slightly sweet flavor reminiscent of anise.

Chives
This herb has a delicate oniony flavor.

Coriander
An intense, aromatic sweet and spicy herb.

coriander

chives

Dill
A pungent, slightly sharp-tasting herb with anise overtones, used widely in Scandinavian, central and eastern-European cooking.

Flat-lcaf parsley
More flavorful than the curly variety, this is a rich source of vitamins and minerals.

Marjoram
Very similar to oregano, though more delicate in flavor. Used widely in Italian cooking.

Mint
One of the most versatile of herbs, with a distinctive scent, mint is used in both sweet and savory dishes.

Oregano
A wild variety of marjoram with a robust flavor.

Rosemary
Use this powerfully aromatic herb sparingly.

Sage
The aromatic oils in sage impart a distinct and powerful flavor, most often found in Italian cooking.

Sorrel
This fresh leafy herb has a sharp acidic flavor.

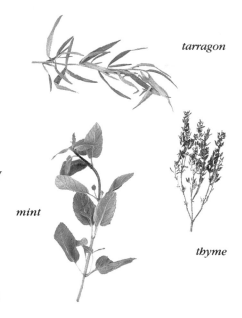

tarragon

mint

thyme

Tarragon
This has a sweet, spicy anise-like flavor.

Thyme
This robust aromatic herb is another vital ingredient of *bouquet garni*.

sorrel

flat-leaf parsley

basil

chervil

Spices and Seasonings

Spices and seasonings are indispensable for enhancing the flavors of foods that might otherwise be bland and lacking in substance.

Allspice
This is available both whole and ground and imparts a flavoring that is like a mixture of nutmeg, cinnamon, cloves and pepper.

Caraway
A pungent and aromatic spice that is widely used in German and Austrian cooking.

Cayenne
Ground from small red chillies, it is extremely spicy, and should be used sparingly.

Cinnamon
Cinnamon is a sweet and fragrant spice ground from the dried, rolled inner bark of a tropical tree that is native to Sri Lanka.

Cloves
A strongly aromatic spice with a slightly bitter taste.

Coriander
A sweet, warm aromatic spice that is used extensively in Indian and South-east Asian cooking.

Cumin
A uniquely flavored spice with a sweetly pungent and very distinctive taste.

Fennel seeds
These seeds have a strong, sweet anise-liquorice flavor.

Ginger
The fresh root has a clean refreshing flavor. Ginger is also available dried and ground.

Green cardamom
The pods should be broken open and the small black seeds ground to fully appreciate the mellow fragrant, slightly spicy aroma.

Juniper berries
These pine-scented, bitter-sweet berries provide the main flavoring of gin.

Lemon grass
A strong clean, refreshing citrus flavoring that is widely used in Thai and Vietnamese cooking.

Nutmeg
A very aromatic spice with a warm, sweet, nutty flavor.

Paprika
The flavor can range from sweet and lightly piquant, to pungent and fiery.

Saffron
This is the most expensive spice in the world, but you need only a tiny amount to flavor and color any dish.

Star anise
A sweet, pungent liquorice-flavored spice that is important in Chinese cooking.

Turmeric
Mainly used for its bright yellow coloring, it has a slightly musty taste and aroma.

Yellow mustard seeds
Less pungent than brown or black mustard seeds, they have a sweet, mild piquancy.

fennel seeds

star anise

cayenne

ginger

green cardamom

ground cloves

cloves

ground nutmeg

nutmeg

ground coriander

coriander seeds

ground cumin

cumin seeds

allspice berries

ground allspice

ground turmeric

ground cinnamon

ground ginger

caraway seeds

juniper berries

yellow mustard seeds

cinnamon sticks

saffron

lemon grass

paprika

Nuts

Nuts provide a healthy source of energy, and are rich in fiber, protein, vitamins B and E and several minerals. However, they are high in fats (though mostly mono- and polyunsaturated) so are usually also high in calories.

pecans

Almonds
There are two types, sweet and bitter, the bitter type being poisonous when eaten raw. This delicious nut enriches many dishes and is especially high in protein.

Brazil nuts
As the name would suggest, these nuts originate from the Brazilian Amazon. The high oil content means that these nuts quickly turn rancid.

Chestnuts
Not to be confused with the horse-chestnut, these softer textured nuts are low in fat and high in carbohydrates. They can be bought fresh, canned (whole or puréed), vacuum-packed and dried.

Hazelnuts
These wonderfully aromatic sweet nuts add flavor to both sweet and savory dishes. Roasting adds more flavor.

Peanuts
Not strictly a true nut, these most popular of nuts have a distinctive flavor and are rich in protein.

Pecans
A native of the USA, these are sweet and richly flavored nuts similar to walnuts.

Pine nuts
These soft, creamy colored nuts are found at the base of a species of pine cone. They have a delicate flavor.

Pistachios
These are richly flavored with a bright green coloring.

Walnuts
The most versatile of all nuts, walnuts impart a rich full flavor.

pistachios

brazil nuts

chestnuts

peanuts

hazelnuts

almonds

pine nuts

walnuts

Flours

Flour can be ground from grains, cereals, seeds, nuts and even roots and tubers.

Buckwheat flour
A non-wheat flour, ground from the seed of a plant that is related to rhubarb. It has a strong nutty flavor and is rich in vitamins A and B, calcium and carbohydrate.

White flour
This contains 75 per cent or less of the wheat grain so is not as nutritious as wholewheat flour.

Wholewheat flour
Ground from the entire whole grain it is rich in protein, vitamins and fibre, so is highly nutritious.

Seeds

Seeds provide a rich source of protein, fiber, vitamins, minerals and starch.

Poppy seeds
These mild, sweet seeds come from the opium poppy, but are free from narcotic properties.

Pumpkin seeds
From the vegetable of the same name, these flat green seeds have a light, distinctive flavor and are rich in zinc, protein and iron.

Sesame seeds
These tiny, light brown or creamy colored seeds have a mild, sweet nutty flavor and are rich in protein and calcium.

Sunflower seeds
These seeds have a distinctive flavor and they are rich in protein, fiber, iron and calcium.

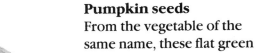

white flour

pumpkin seeds

poppy seeds

buckwheat flour

sunflower seeds

sesame seeds

wholewheat flour

TECHNIQUES

Once mastered, the techniques described here will help you to prepare
vegetables speedily and with less waste, to produce better results with ease.

Peeling and Seeding Tomatoes

A simple and efficient way of preparing tomatoes.

1 Use a sharp knife to cut a small cross on the bottom of the tomato.

2 Turn the tomato over and cut out the core.

3 Immerse the tomato in boiling water for 10–15 seconds, then transfer to a bowl of cold water using a slotted spoon.

4 Lift out the tomato and peel (the skin should be easy to remove).

5 Cut the tomato in half crosswise and squeeze out the seeds.

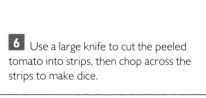

6 Use a large knife to cut the peeled tomato into strips, then chop across the strips to make dice.

Chopping Onions

Uniform-sized dice make cooking easy. This method can't be beaten.

1 Peel the onion. Cut it in half with a large knife and set it cut-side down on a board. Make lengthwise vertical cuts along the onion, cutting almost but not quite through to the root.

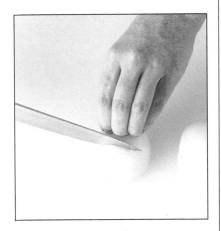

2 Make 2 horizontal cuts from the stalk and towards the root, but not through it.

3 Cut the onion crosswise to form small, even dice.

Slicing Onions

Use thin slices for sautéeing or to flavor oils for stir-frying, or use sweet onion slices in salads.

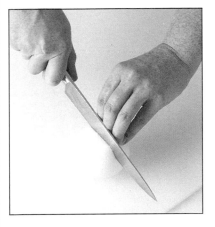

1 Peel the onion. Cut it in half with a large knife and set it cut-side down on a chopping board.

2 Cut out a triangular piece of the core from each half.

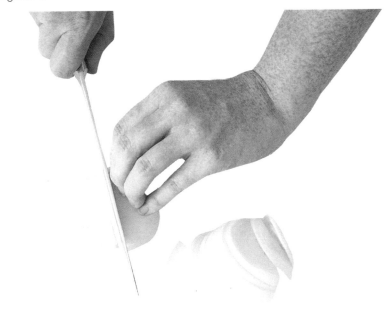

3 Cut across each half in vertical slices.

Shredding Cabbage

This method is useful for coleslaws, pickled cabbage or any cooked dish.

1 Use a large knife to cut the cabbage into quarters.

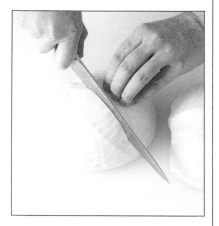

2 Cut out the core from each quarter.

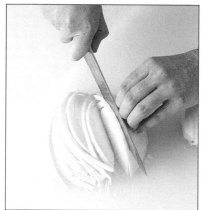

3 Slice across each quarter to form fine, even shreds.

Cutting Carrot Julienne

Thin julienne strips of any vegetable make decorative accompaniments, or can be used in stir-fries.

1 Peel the carrot and use a large knife to cut it into 2 in lengths. Cut a thin sliver from one side of each piece so that it sits flat on the board.

2 Cut into thin lengthwise slices.

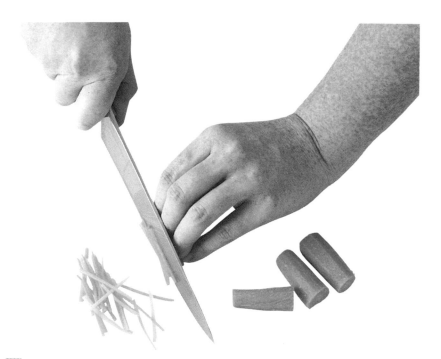

3 Stack the slices and cut through them to make fine strips.

Chopping Fresh Ginger

Fresh ginger imparts a clean, refreshing taste. Follow the instructions to chop finely.

1 Break off small knobs of ginger from the main root and peel.

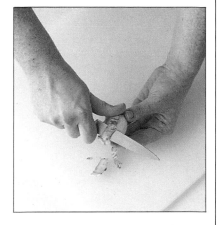

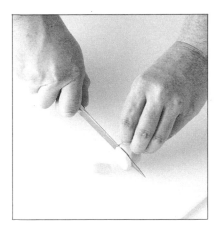

2 Slice lengthwise and cut into strips.

3 Cut across the strips to form small, even dice.

Chopping Chillies

Fresh chillics must be handled with care. Always work in a well-ventilated area and keep away from your eyes.

1 Cut the chilli in half lengthwise and remove the core and seeds.

2 Cut it into lengthwise strips.

3 Cut across the strips to form small, even dice.

Melon and Basil Soup

A deliciously refreshing, chilled fruit soup, just right for a hot summer's day.

Serves 4–6

INGREDIENTS
2 canteloupe or honeydew melons
1/3 cup superfine sugar
3/4 cup water
finely grated zest and juice of 1 lime
3 tbsp shredded fresh basil
fresh basil leaves, to garnish

basil

sugar

lime

melon

1 Cut the melons in half across the middle. Scrape out the seeds and discard. Using a melon baller, scoop out 20–24 balls and set aside for the garnish. Scoop out the remaining flesh and place in a blender or food processor.

2 Place the sugar, water and lime zest in a small pan over a low heat. Stir until dissolved, bring to the boil and simmer for 2–3 minutes. Remove from the heat and leave to cool slightly. Pour half the mixture into the blender or food processor with the melon flesh. Blend until smooth, adding the remaining syrup and lime juice to taste.

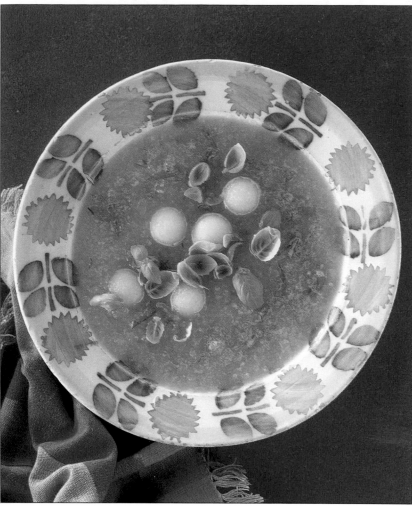

COOK'S TIP

Add the syrup in two stages, as the amount of sugar needed will depend on the sweetness of the melon.

3 Pour the mixture into a bowl, stir in the basil and chill. Serve garnished with basil leaves and melon balls.

Leek, Parsnip and Ginger Soup

A flavorful winter warmer, with the added spiciness of fresh ginger.

Serves 4–6

INGREDIENTS
2 tbsp olive oil
8 oz leeks, sliced
2 tbsp finely chopped fresh ginger root
1½ lb parsnips, roughly chopped
1¼ cups dry white wine, such as Sauvignon blanc
5 cups vegetable stock or water
salt and freshly ground black pepper
low-fat ricotta cheese, to garnish
paprika, to garnish

ginger

parsnip

vegetable stock

leeks

1 Heat the oil in a large pan and add the leeks and ginger. Cook gently for 2–3 minutes, until the leeks start to soften.

2 Add the parsnips and cook for a further 7–8 minutes.

3 Pour in the wine and stock or water and bring to the boil. Reduce the heat and simmer for 20–30 minutes or until the parsnips are tender.

4 Purée in a blender until smooth. Season to taste. Reheat and garnish with a swirl of ricotta cheese and a light dusting of paprika.

Chilled Fresh Tomato Soup

This effortless uncooked soup can be made in minutes.

Serves 4–6

INGREDIENTS

3–3½ lb ripe tomatoes, peeled and
    roughly chopped
4 garlic cloves, crushed
2 tbsp extra-virgin olive oil (optional)
2 tbsp balsamic vinegar
freshly ground black pepper
4 slices wholewheat bread
low-fat ricotta cheese, to garnish

wholewheat bread

garlic

ricotta cheese

peppercorns

tomato

COOK'S TIP

For the best flavor, it is important to use only fully ripened, succulent tomatoes in this soup.

1 Place the tomatoes in a blender with the garlic and olive oil if using. Blend until smooth.

2 Pass the mixture through a sieve to remove the seeds. Stir in the balsamic vinegar and season to taste with pepper. Leave in the fridge to chill.

3 Toast the bread lightly on both sides. While still hot, cut off the crusts and slice in half horizontally. Place the toast on a board with the uncooked sides facing down and, using a circular motion, rub to remove any doughy pieces of bread.

4 Cut each slice into 4 triangles. Place on a griddle and toast the uncooked sides until lightly golden. Garnish each bowl of soup with a spoonful of ricotta cheese and serve with the melba toast.

Broccoli and Almond Soup

The creaminess of the toasted almonds combines perfectly with the slight bitterness of the taste of broccoli.

Serves 4–6

INGREDIENTS
⅔ cup ground almonds
1½ lb broccoli
3¾ cups fresh vegetable stock or
    water
1¼ cups skim or low-fat milk
salt and freshly ground black pepper

ground almonds

skim milk

broccoli

1 Preheat the oven to 350°F. Spread the ground almonds evenly on a cookie sheet and toast in the oven for about 10 minutes, or until just golden. Reserve ¼ of the almonds and set aside for the garnish.

2 Cut the broccoli into small florets and steam for 6–7 minutes or until tender.

3 Place the remaining toasted almonds, broccoli, stock or water and milk in a blender and blend until smooth. Season to taste.

4 Reheat the soup and serve sprinkled with the reserved toasted almonds.

Red Onion and Beet Soup

This beautiful vivid ruby-red soup will look stunning at any dinner party.

Serves 4–6

INGREDIENTS
1 tbsp olive oil
12 oz red onions, sliced
2 garlic cloves, crushed
10 oz cooked beets, cut into
   thin sticks
5 cups fresh vegetable stock or water
1 cup cooked soup pasta
2 tbsp raspberry vinegar
salt and freshly ground black pepper
low-fat yogurt or ricotta cheese, to
   garnish
snipped chives, to garnish

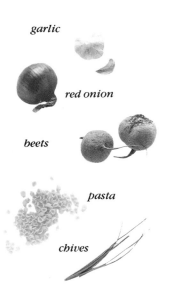

garlic

red onion

beets

pasta

chives

1 Heat the olive oil and add the onions and garlic.

2 Cook gently for about 20 minutes or until soft and tender.

3 Add the beets, stock or water, cooked pasta shapes and vinegar and heat through. Season to taste.

4 Ladle into bowls. Top each one with a spoonful of yogurt or ricotta cheese and sprinkle with chives.

COOK'S TIP

Try substituting cooked barley for the pasta to give extra nuttiness.

Cauliflower, Flageolet and Fennel Seed Soup

The sweet, anise-liquorice flavor of the fennel seeds gives a delicious edge to this hearty soup.

Serves 4–6

INGREDIENTS
1 tbsp olive oil
1 garlic clove, crushed
1 onion, chopped
2 tsp fennel seeds
1 cauliflower, cut into small florets
2 × 14 oz cans flageolet beans, drained and rinsed
5 cups fresh vegetable stock or water
salt and freshly ground black pepper
chopped fresh parsley, to garnish
toasted slices of French bread, to serve

flageolet beans

French bread

onion

garlic

cauliflower

fennel seeds

parsley

1 Heat the olive oil. Add the garlic, onion and fennel seeds and cook gently for 5 minutes or until softened.

2 Add the cauliflower, half of the beans and the stock or water.

3 Bring to a boil. Reduce the heat and simmer for 10 minutes or until the cauliflower is tender.

4 Pour the soup into a blender and blend until smooth. Stir in the remaining beans and season to taste. Reheat and pour into bowls. Sprinkle with chopped parsley and serve with toasted slices of French bread.

Cucumber and Alfalfa Tortillas

Wheat tortillas are extremely simple to prepare at home. Served with a crisp, fresh salsa, they make a marvelous light lunch or supper dish.

COOK'S TIP

When peeling the avocado be sure to scrape off the bright green flesh from immediately under the skin as this gives the sauce its vivid green color.

Serves 4

INGREDIENTS
2 cups flour, sifted
pinch of salt
3 tbsp olive oil
½–⅔ cup warm water
lime wedges, to garnish

FOR THE SALSA
1 red onion, finely chopped
1 fresh red chilli, seeded and finely
   chopped
2 tbsp chopped fresh dill or coriander
½ cucumber, peeled and chopped
6 oz alfalfa sprouts

FOR THE SAUCE
1 large ripe avocado, peeled and
   pitted
juice of 1 lime
2 tbsp soft goat cheese
pinch of paprika

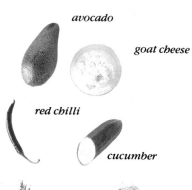
avocado

goat cheese

red chilli

cucumber

dill   *alfalfa sprouts*

1 Mix all the salsa ingredients together in a bowl and set aside.

2 To make the sauce, place the avocado, lime juice and goat cheese in a food processor or blender and blend until smooth. Place in a bowl and cover with plastic wrap. Dust with paprika just before serving.

3 To make the tortillas, place the flour and salt in a food processor, add the oil and blend. Gradually add the water (the amount will vary depending on the type of flour). Stop adding water when a stiff dough has formed. Turn out onto a floured board and knead until smooth. Cover with a damp cloth.

4 Divide the mixture into 8 pieces. Knead each piece for a couple of minutes and form into a ball. Flatten and roll out each ball to a 9 in circle.

5 Heat an ungreased cast-iron pan. Cook 1 tortilla at a time for about 30 seconds on each side. Place the cooked tortillas in a clean dish-towel and repeat until you have 8 tortillas.

6 To serve, spread each tortilla with a spoonful of avocado sauce, top with salsa and roll up. Garnish with lime wedges.

Baked Herb Crêpes

These mouth-watering, light herb crêpes make a striking starter at a dinner party, but are equally splendid served with a crisp salad for lunch.

Serves 4

INGREDIENTS
2 tbsp chopped fresh herbs
   (e.g. parsley, thyme, and chervil)
1 tbsp sunflower oil, plus extra for
   frying
½ cup skim milk
3 eggs
¼ cup flour
pinch of salt
1 tbsp olive oil

FOR THE SAUCE
2 tbsp olive oil
1 small onion, chopped
2 garlic cloves, crushed
1 tbsp grated fresh ginger root
1 × 14 oz can chopped tomatoes

FOR THE FILLING
1 lb fresh spinach
¾ cup ricotta cheese
2 tbsp pine nuts, toasted
5 halves sun-dried tomatoes in olive
   oil, drained and chopped
2 tbsp shredded fresh basil
salt, nutmeg and freshly ground black
   pepper
4 egg whites

1 To make the crêpes, place the herbs and oil in a blender and blend until smooth, pushing down any whole pieces with a spatula. Add the milk, eggs, flour and salt and process again until smooth and pale green. Leave to rest for 30 minutes.

onion

parsley

ginger root

chopped tomatoes

spinach

sun-dried tomatoes

garlic

nutmeg

thyme

flour

egg

skim milk

2 Heat a small non-stick crêpe or frying pan and add a very small amount of oil. Pour out any excess oil and pour in a ladleful of the batter. Swirl around to cover the base. Cook for 1–2 minutes, turn over and cook the other side. Repeat with the remaining batter to make 8 crêpes.

3 To make the sauce, heat the oil in a small pan. Add the onion, garlic and ginger and cook gently for 5 minutes until softened. Add the tomatoes and cook for a further 10–15 minutes until the mixture thickens. Purée in a blender, sieve and set aside.

4 To make the filling, wash the spinach, removing any large stalks, and place in a large pan with only the water that clings to the leaves. Cover and cook, stirring once, until the spinach has just wilted. Remove from the heat and refresh in cold water. Place in a sieve or colander, squeeze out the excess water and chop finely. Mix the spinach with the ricotta, pine nuts, sun-dried tomatoes and basil. Season with salt, nutmeg and freshly ground black pepper.

5 Preheat the oven to 375°F. Whisk the 4 egg whites until they form stiff peaks but are not dry. Fold ⅓ into the spinach and ricotta to lighten the mixture, then gently fold in the rest.

6 Taking one crêpe at a time, place on a lightly oiled cookie sheet. Place a large spoonful of filling on each one and fold into quarters. Repeat until all the filling and crêpes are used up. Bake in the oven for 10–15 minutes or until set. Reheat the tomato sauce to serve with the crêpes.

COOK'S TIP
If preferred, use plain sun-dried tomatoes without any oil, and soak them in warm water for 20 minutes before using.

Buckwheat Blinis

These delectable light pancakes originated in Russia. For a special occasion, serve with a small glass of chilled vodka.

Serves 4

INGREDIENTS
1 tsp easy-blend dry yeast
1 cup skim or low-fat milk, warmed
⅓ cup buckwheat flour
⅓ cup flour
2 tsp sugar
pinch of salt
1 egg, separated
oil, for frying

FOR THE AVOCADO CREAM
1 large avocado
⅓ cup low-fat ricotta cheese
juice of 1 lime

FOR THE PICKLED BEETS
8 oz beets
3 tbsp lime juice
snipped chives, to garnish
cracked black peppercorns, to garnish

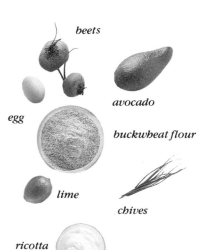

beets

avocado

egg

buckwheat flour

lime

chives

ricotta cheese

skim milk

1 Mix the dry yeast with the milk, then mix with the next 4 ingredients and the egg yolk. Cover with a cloth and leave to prove for about 40 minutes. Whisk the egg white until stiff but not dry and fold into the blini mixture.

2 Heat a little oil in a non-stick pan and add a ladleful of batter to make a 4 in pancake. Cook for 2–3 minutes on each side. Repeat with the remaining batter mixture to make 8 blinis.

3 Cut the avocado in half and remove the pit. Peel and place the flesh in a blender with the ricotta cheese and lime juice. Blend until smooth.

4 Peel the beets and shred finely. Mix with the lime juice. To serve, top each blini with a spoonful of avocado cream. Serve with the pickled beets and garnish with snipped chives and cracked black peppercorns.

Cheese-stuffed Pears

These pears, with their scrumptious creamy topping, make a sublime dish when served with a simple salad.

Serves 4

INGREDIENTS
¼ cup ricotta cheese
¼ cup Saga blue cheese
1 tbsp honey
½ celery stalk, finely sliced
8 green olives, pitted and roughly
   chopped
4 dates, pitted and cut into thin strips
pinch of paprika
4 ripe pears
⅔ cup apple juice

honey

pear

apple juice

dates

Saga blue

celery

olives

COOK'S TIP
Choose ripe pears in season such as Bartlett or Comice.

1 Preheat the oven to 400°F. Place the ricotta in a bowl and crumble in the Saga blue cheese. Add the rest of the ingredients except for the pears and apple juice and mix well.

2 Halve the pears lengthwise and use a melon baller to remove the cores. Place in a ovenproof dish and divide the filling equally between them.

3 Pour in the apple juice and cover the dish with foil. Bake for 20 minutes or until the pears are tender.

4 Remove the foil and place the dish under a hot broiler for 3 minutes. Serve immediately.

Soufflé Omelette

This delectable soufflé omelette is light and delicate enough to melt in your mouth.

Serves 1

INGREDIENTS
2 eggs, separated
2 tbsp cold water
1 tbsp chopped fresh coriander
salt and freshly ground black pepper
½ tbsp olive oil
2 tbsp mango chutney
¼ cup Jarlsberg or Swiss cheese, grated

Jarlsberg

mango chutney

eggs

coriander

COOK'S TIP

A light hand is essential to the success of this dish. Do not overmix the egg whites into the yolks or the mixture will be heavy.

1 Beat the egg yolks together with the cold water, coriander and seasoning.

2 Whisk the egg whites until stiff but not dry and gently fold into the egg yolk mixture.

3 Heat the oil in a frying pan, pour in the egg mixture and reduce the heat. Do not stir. Cook until the omelette becomes puffy and golden brown on the underside (carefully lift one edge with a spatula to check).

4 Spoon on the chutney and sprinkle on the Jarlsberg. Fold over and slide onto a warm plate. Eat immediately. (If preferred, before adding the chutney and cheese, place the pan under a hot broiler to set the top.)

Nutty Cheese Balls

An extremely quick and simple recipe. Try making a smaller version to serve as canapés at a drinks party.

Serves 4

INGREDIENTS
1 cup low-fat ricotta cheese
¼ cup Saga blue cheese
1 tbsp finely chopped onion
1 tbsp finely chopped celery stalk
1 tbsp finely chopped parsley
1 tbsp finely chopped gherkin
1 tsp brandy or port (optional)
pinch of paprika
½ cup walnuts or pecans, roughly
    chopped
6 tbsp snipped chives
salt and freshly ground black pepper

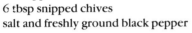

celery

Saga blue cheese

gherkins

ricotta cheese

onion

walnuts

chives

parsley

paprika

1 Beat the ricotta cheese and Saga blue together using a spoon.

2 Mix in all the remaining ingredients except the snipped chives.

3 Divide the mixture into 12 pieces and roll into balls.

4 Roll each ball gently in the snipped chives. Leave in the fridge to chill for about an hour before serving.

Sweet Potato Roulade

Sweet potato works particularly well as the base for this roulade. Serve in thin slices for a truly impressive dinner party dish.

Serves 6

INGREDIENTS
1 cup low-fat ricotta cheese
5 tbsp low-fat yogurt
6–8 scallions, finely sliced
2 tbsp chopped brazil nuts, roasted
1 lb sweet potatoes, peeled and
    coarsely cubed
12 allspice berries, crushed
4 eggs, separated
¼ cup Edam or Gouda cheese, finely
    grated
salt and freshly ground black pepper
1 tbsp sesame seeds

yogurt

sesame seeds

sweet potato

ricotta cheese

Edam

brazil nuts

scallions

peppercorns

egg

1 Preheat the oven to 400°F. Grease and line a 13 × 10 in jelly roll pan with parchment paper, snipping the corners with scissors to fit neatly into the pan.

2 In a small bowl, mix together the ricotta, yogurt, scallions and brazil nuts. Set aside.

3 Boil or steam the sweet potato until tender. Drain well. Place in a food processor with the allspice and blend until smooth. Spoon into a bowl and stir in the egg yolks and Edam. Season to taste.

4 Whisk the egg whites until stiff but not dry. Fold ⅓ of the egg whites into the sweet potatoes to lighten the mixture before gently folding in the rest.

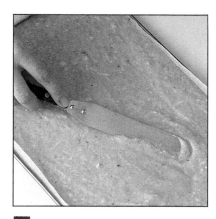

5 Pour into the prepared pan, tipping it to get the mixture right into the corners. Smooth gently with a spatula and cook in the oven for 10–15 minutes.

COOK'S TIP

Choose the orange-fleshed variety of sweet potato for the most striking color.

6 Meanwhile, lay a large sheet of waxed paper on a clean dish-towel and sprinkle with the sesame seeds. When the roulade is cooked, tip it onto the paper, trim the edges and roll it up. Leave to cool. When cool carefully unroll, spread with the filling and roll up again. Cut into slices to serve.

Pumpkin and Pistachio Risotto

This elegant combination of creamy golden rice and orange pumpkin can be as pale or bright as you like by adding different quantities of saffron.

Serves 4

INGREDIENTS

5 cups fresh vegetable stock or water
generous pinch of saffron threads
2 tbsp olive oil
1 medium onion, chopped
2 garlic cloves, crushed
1 lb arborio rice
2 lb pumpkin, peeled, seeded and cut
   into ¾ in cubes
¾ cup dry white wine
½ oz Parmesan cheese, finely grated
½ cup pistachios
3 tbsp chopped fresh marjoram or
   oregano, plus extra leaves, to
   garnish
salt, freshly grated nutmeg and ground
   black pepper

2 Heat the oil in a large saucepan. Add the onion and garlic and cook gently for about 5 minutes until softened. Add the rice and pumpkin and cook for a few more minutes until the rice looks transparent.

3 Pour in the wine and allow it to boil hard. When it is absorbed add ¼ of the stock and the infused saffron and liquid. Stir constantly until all the liquid is absorbed.

1 Bring the stock or water to a boil and reduce to a low simmer. Ladle a little stock into a small bowl. Add the saffron threads and leave to infuse.

4 Gradually add the stock or water, a ladleful at a time, allowing the rice to absorb the liquid before adding more and stirring all the time. After 20–30 minutes the rice should be golden yellow and creamy, and *al dente* when tested.

saffron

pumpkin

white wine

onion

garlic

marjoram

Parmesan

arborio rice

pistachios

5 Stir in the Parmesan cheese, cover the pan and leave to stand for 5 minutes.

6 To finish, stir in the pistachios and marjoram or oregano. Season to taste with a little salt, nutmeg and pepper, and scatter over a few extra marjoram or oregano leaves.

COOK'S TIP

Italian arborio rice must be used to make an authentic risotto. Choose unpolished white arborio as it contains more starch.

Wild Rice Rösti with Carrot and Orange Purée

Rösti is a traditional dish from Switzerland. This variation has the extra nuttiness of wild rice and a bright simple sauce as a fresh accompaniment.

Serves 6

INGREDIENTS
½ cup wild rice
2 lb large potatoes
3 tbsp walnut oil
1 tsp yellow mustard seeds
1 onion, coarsely grated and drained in a sieve
2 tbsp fresh thyme leaves
salt and freshly ground black pepper

FOR THE PURÉE
12 oz carrots, peeled and roughly chopped
rind and juice of 1 large orange

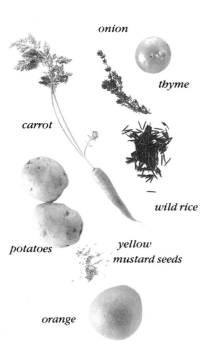

onion
thyme
carrot
wild rice
potatoes
yellow mustard seeds
orange

1 For the purée, place the carrots in a pan, cover with cold water and add 2 pieces of orange rind. Bring to a boil and cook for 10 minutes or until tender. Drain well and discard the rind.

2 Purée the mixture in a blender with 4 tbsp of the orange juice. Return to the pan to reheat.

3 Place the wild rice in a clean pan and cover with water. Bring to a boil and cook for 30–40 minutes, until the rice is just starting to split, but still crunchy. Drain the rice.

4 Scrub the potatoes, place in a large pan and cover with cold water. Bring to a boil and cook for 10–15 minutes until just tender. Drain well and leave to cool slightly. When the potatoes are cool, peel and coarsely grate them into a large bowl. Add the cooked rice.

5 Heat 2 tbsp of the walnut oil in a non-stick frying pan and add the mustard seeds. When they start to pop, add the onion and cook gently for 5 minutes until softened. Add to the bowl of potato and rice, together with the thyme, and mix thoroughly. Season to taste with salt and pepper.

6 Heat the remaining oil in the frying pan and add the potato mixture. Press down well and cook for 10 minutes or until golden brown. Cover the pan with a plate and flip over, then slide the rösti back into the pan for another 10 minutes to cook the other side. Serve with the reheated carrot and orange purée.

Thai Fragrant Rice

A lovely, soft, fluffy rice dish, perfumed with fresh lemon grass.

Serves 4

INGREDIENTS
1 piece of lemon grass
2 limes
1 cup brown basmati rice
1 tbsp olive oil
1 onion, chopped
1 in piece of fresh ginger root, peeled and finely chopped
1½ tsp coriander seeds
1½ tsp cumin seeds
3 cups fresh vegetable stock or water
4 tbsp chopped fresh coriander
lime wedges, to serve

onion

lime

ginger

lemon grass

coriander seeds

basmati rice

cumin seeds

coriander

1 Finely chop the lemon grass.

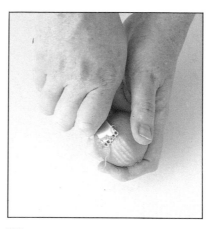

2 Remove the zest from the limes using a zester or fine grater.

3 Rinse the rice in plenty of cold water until the water runs clear. Drain through a sieve.

4 Heat the oil in a large pan and add the onion and spices, lemon grass and lime zest and cook gently for 2–3 minutes.

5 Add the rice and cook for another minute, then add the stock and bring to a boil. Reduce the heat to very low and cover the pan. Cook gently for 30 minutes then check the rice. If it is still crunchy, cover the pan again and leave for a further 3–5 minutes. Remove from the heat.

6 Stir in the fresh coriander, fluff up the grains, cover and leave for 10 minutes. Serve with lime wedges.

COOK'S TIP

Other varieties of rice, such as white basmati or long grain, can be used for this dish but you will need to adjust the cooking times accordingly.

Sweet Vegetable Couscous

A wonderful combination of sweet vegetables and spices, this makes a substantial winter dish.

Serves 4–6

INGREDIENTS
1 generous pinch of saffron threads
3 tbsp boiling water
1 tbsp olive oil
1 red onion, sliced
2 garlic, cloves
1–2 fresh red chillies, seeded and finely chopped
½ tsp ground ginger
½ tsp ground cinnamon
1 × 400 g/14 oz can chopped tomatoes
1¼ cups fresh vegetable stock or water
4 medium carrots, peeled and cut into ¼ in slices
2 medium turnips, peeled and cut into ¾ in cubes
1 lb sweet potatoes, peeled and cut into ¾ in cubes
⅓ cup raisins
2 medium zucchini, cut into ¼ in slices
1 × 14 oz can chick-peas, drained and rinsed
3 tbsp chopped fresh parsley
3 tbsp chopped fresh coriander
1 lb quick-cooking couscous

1 Leave the saffron to infuse in the boiling water.

2 Heat the oil in a large saucepan. Add the onion, garlic and chillies and cook gently for 5 minutes.

3 Add the ground ginger and cinnamon and cook for a further 1–2 minutes.

4 Add the tomatoes, stock or water, infused saffron and liquid, carrots, turnips, sweet potatoes and raisins, cover and simmer for 25 minutes.

red onion

chick-peas

couscous

chopped tomatoes

zucchini

carrot

red chilli

garlic

turnip

raisins

sweet potato

5 Add the zucchini, chick-peas, parsley and coriander and cook for another 10 minutes.

6 Meanwhile prepare the couscous following the package instructions and serve with the vegetables.

Lemon and Ginger Spicy Beans

An extremely quick delicious meal, made with canned beans for speed. You probably won't need extra salt as canned beans tend to be already salted.

Serves 4

INGREDIENTS
2 tbsp roughly chopped fresh ginger
  root
3 garlic cloves, roughly chopped
1 cup cold water
1 tbsp sunflower oil
1 large onion, thinly sliced
1 fresh red chilli, seeded and finely
  chopped
¼ tsp cayenne pepper
2 tsp ground cumin
1 tsp ground coriander
½ tsp ground turmeric
2 tbsp lemon juice
⅓ cup chopped fresh coriander
1 × 14 oz can black-eyed beans,
  drained and rinsed
1 × 14 oz can adzuki beans, drained
  and rinsed
1 × 14 oz can navy beans, drained and
  rinsed
freshly ground black pepper

1 Place the ginger, garlic and 4 tbsp of the cold water in a blender and mix until smooth.

garlic

red chilli

adzuki beans

ginger

black-eyed beans

ground coriander

ground turmeric

ground cumin

navy beans

onion

2 Heat the oil in a pan. Add the onion and chilli and cook gently for 5 minutes until softened.

3 Add the cayenne pepper, cumin, ground coriander and turmeric and stir-fry for 1 minute.

4 Stir in the ginger and garlic paste from the blender and cook for another minute.

5 Add the remaining water, lemon juice and fresh coriander, stir well and bring to a boil. Cover the pan tightly and cook for 5 minutes.

6 Add all the beans and cook for a further 5–10 minutes. Season with pepper to taste and serve.

Green Lentil and Cabbage Salad

This warm crunchy salad makes a satisfying meal if served with crusty French bread or wholemeal rolls.

Serves 4–6

INGREDIENTS
1 cup green lentils
6 cups cold water
1 garlic clove
1 bay leaf
1 small onion, peeled and studded
    with 2 cloves
1 tbsp olive oil
1 red onion, finely sliced
2 garlic cloves, crushed
1 tbsp thyme leaves
12 oz cabbage, finely shredded
finely grated rind and juice of 1 lemon
1 tbsp raspberry vinegar
salt and freshly ground black pepper

thyme

cabbage

onion

red onion

bay leaf

lemon

garlic

cloves

peppercorns

1 Rinse the lentils in cold water and place in a large pan with the water, peeled garlic clove, bay leaf and clove-studded onion. Bring to a boil and cook for 10 minutes. Reduce the heat, cover the pan and simmer gently for 15–20 minutes. Drain and remove the onion, garlic and bay leaf.

2 Heat the oil in a large pan. Add the red onion, garlic and thyme and cook for 5 minutes until softened.

3 Add the cabbage and cook for 3–5 minutes until just cooked but still crunchy.

4 Stir in the cooked lentils, lemon rind and juice and the raspberry vinegar. Season to taste and serve.

Polenta and Baked Tomatoes

A staple of northern Italy, polenta is a nourishing, filling food, served here with a delicious fresh tomato and olive topping.

Serves 4–6

INGREDIENTS
9 cups water
1¼ lb quick-cooking polenta
12 large ripe plum tomatoes, sliced
4 garlic cloves, thinly sliced
2 tbsp chopped fresh oregano or
    marjoram
½ cup black olives, pitted
salt and freshly ground black pepper
2 tbsp olive oil

black olives

marjoram

plum tomatoes

garlic

oregano

polenta

1 Place the water in a large saucepan and bring to a boil. Whisk in the polenta and simmer for 5 minutes.

2 Remove the pan from the heat and pour the thickened polenta into a 9 in × 13 in jelly roll pan. Smooth out the surface with a spatula until level, and leave to cool.

3 Preheat the oven to 350°F. With a 3 in round pastry cutter, stamp out 12 rounds of polenta. Lay them so that they slightly overlap in a lightly oiled ovenproof dish.

4 Layer the tomatoes, garlic, oregano or marjoram and olives on top of the polenta, seasoning the layers as you go. Sprinkle with the olive oil, and bake uncovered for 30–35 minutes. Serve immediately.

Sesame Noodle Salad with Hot Peanuts

An orient-inspired salad with crunchy vegetables and a light soy dressing. The hot peanuts make a surprisingly successful union with the cold noodles.

Serves 4

INGREDIENTS
12 oz egg noodles
2 carrots, peeled and cut into fine
   julienne strips
½ cucumber, peeled and cut into
   ½ in cubes
4 oz celeriac, peeled and cut into fine
   julienne strips
6 scallions, finely sliced
8 canned water chestnuts, drained
   and finely sliced
6 oz beansprouts
1 small fresh green chilli, seeded and
   finely chopped
2 tbsp sesame seeds, to serve
1 cup peanuts, to serve

FOR THE DRESSING
1 tbsp dark soy sauce
1 tbsp light soy sauce
1 tbsp honey
1 tbsp rice wine or dry sherry
1 tbsp sesame oil

1 Preheat the oven to 400°F. Cook the egg noodles in boiling water, following the instructions on the side of the package.

2 Drain the noodles, refresh in cold water, then drain again.

3 Mix the noodles with all of the prepared vegetables.

sesame seeds

beansprouts   *green chilli*   *scallion*

celeriac

water chestnuts   *cucumber*   *peanuts*   *noodles*

carrot

4 Combine the dressing ingredients in a small bowl, then toss into the noodle and vegetable mixture. Divide the salad between 4 plates.

5 Place the sesame seeds and peanuts on separate cookie sheets and place in the oven. Take the sesame seeds out after 5 minutes and continue to cook the peanuts for a further 5 minutes until evenly browned.

6 Sprinkle the sesame seeds and peanuts evenly over each portion and serve at once.

Penne with Eggplant and Mint Pesto

This splendid variation on the classic Italian pesto uses fresh mint rather than basil for a different flavor.

Serves 4

INGREDIENTS
2 large eggplants
salt
1 lb penne
2 oz walnut halves

FOR THE PESTO
1 oz fresh mint
½ oz flat-leaf parsley
1½ oz walnuts
1½ oz Parmesan cheese, finely grated
2 garlic cloves
6 tbsp olive oil
salt and freshly ground black pepper

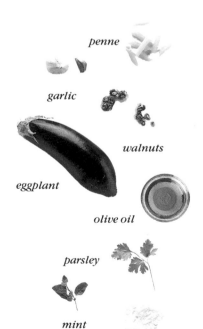

penne

garlic

walnuts

eggplant

olive oil

parsley

mint

Parmesan

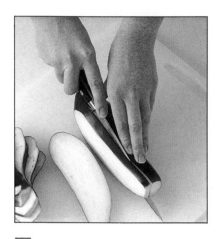

1 Cut the eggplants lengthwise into 1 cm/½ in slices.

2 Cut the slices again crosswise to give short strips.

3 Layer the strips in a colander with salt and leave to stand for 30 minutes over a plate to catch any juices. Rinse well in cool water and drain.

4 Place all the pesto ingredients except the oil in a blender or food processor, blend until smooth, then gradually add the oil in a thin stream until the mixture comes together. Season to taste.

5 Cook the penne following the instructions on the side of the package for about 8 minutes or until nearly cooked. Add the eggplant and cook for a further 3 minutes.

6 Drain well and mix in the mint pesto and walnut halves. Serve immediately.

Campanelle with Yellow Pepper Sauce

Roasted yellow peppers make a deliciously sweet and creamy sauce to serve with pasta.

Serves 4

INGREDIENTS
2 yellow peppers
¼ cup soft goat cheese
½ cup low-fat ricotta cheese
salt and freshly ground black pepper
1 lb short pasta such as campanelle or fusilli
¼ cup flaked almonds, toasted, to serve

pepper

ricotta cheese

flaked almonds

goat cheese

campanelle

1 Place the whole yellow peppers under a preheated grill until charred and blistered. Place in a paper bag to cool. Peel and remove the seeds.

2 Place the pepper flesh in a blender with the goat cheese and ricotta cheese. Blend until smooth. Season with salt and lots of black pepper.

3 Cook the pasta following the instructions on the side of the package until *al dente*. Drain well.

4 Toss with the sauce and serve sprinkled with the toasted flaked almonds.

Spaghetti with Black Olive and Mushroom Sauce

A rich pungent sauce topped with sweet cherry tomatoes.

Serves 4

INGREDIENTS
1 tbsp olive oil
1 garlic clove, chopped
8 oz mushrooms, chopped
Generous ½ cup black olives, pitted
2 tbsp chopped fresh parsley
1 fresh red chilli, seeded and chopped
1 lb spaghetti
8 oz cherry tomatoes
slivers of Parmesan cheese, to serve
   (optional)

garlic

mushrooms

red chillies

cherry tomatoes

spaghetti

black olives

parsley

1 Heat the oil in a large pan. Add the garlic and cook for 1 minute. Add the mushrooms, cover, and cook over a medium heat for 5 minutes.

2 Place the mushrooms in a blender or food processor with the olives, parsley and red chilli. Blend until smooth.

3 Cook the pasta following the instructions on the side of the package until *al dente*. Drain well and return to the pan. Add the olive mixture and toss together until the pasta is well coated. Cover and keep warm.

4 Heat an ungreased frying pan and shake the cherry tomatoes around until they start to split (about 2–3 minutes). Serve the pasta topped with the tomatoes and garnished with slivers of Parmesan, if desired.

Tagliatelle with Pea Sauce, Asparagus and Broad Beans

A creamy pea sauce makes a wonderful combination with the crunchy young vegetables.

Serves 4

INGREDIENTS
1 tbsp olive oil
1 garlic clove, crushed
6 scallions, sliced
1 cup fresh or frozen baby peas,
     defrosted
12 oz fresh young asparagus
2 tbsp chopped fresh sage, plus extra
     leaves, to garnish
finely grated rind of 2 lemons
1¾ cups fresh vegetable stock or
     water
8 oz fresh or frozen broad beans,
     defrosted
1 lb tagliatelle
4 tbsp low-fat yogurt

lemon

garlic

asparagus

broad beans

peas

yogurt *tagliatelle*

sage

scallions

1 Heat the oil in a pan. Add the garlic and scallions and cook gently for 2–3 minutes until softened.

2 Add the peas and ⅓ of the asparagus, together with the sage, lemon rind and stock or water. Bring to a boil, reduce the heat and simmer for 10 minutes until tender. Purée in a blender until smooth.

3 Meanwhile remove the outer skins from the broad beans and discard.

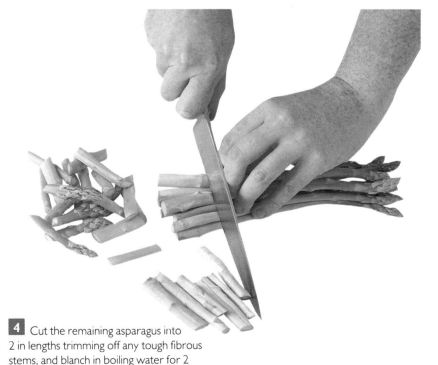

4 Cut the remaining asparagus into 2 in lengths trimming off any tough fibrous stems, and blanch in boiling water for 2 minutes.

5 Cook the tagliatelle following the instructions on the side of the package until *al dente*. Drain well.

COOK'S TIP

Frozen peas and beans have been
suggested here to cut down the
preparation time, but the dish tastes
even better if you use fresh young
vegetables when in season.

6 Add the cooked asparagus and
shelled beans to the sauce and reheat. Stir
in the yogurt and toss into the tagliatelle.
Garnish with a few extra sage leaves and
serve.

Coriander Ravioli with Pumpkin filling

A stunning herb pasta with a superb creamy pumpkin and roast garlic filling.

Serves 4–6

INGREDIENTS
scant 1 cup flour
2 eggs
pinch of salt
3 tbsp chopped fresh coriander
coriander sprigs, to garnish

FOR THE FILLING
4 garlic cloves in their skins
1 lb pumpkin, peeled and seeds
    removed
½ cup ricotta cheese
4 halves sun-dried tomatoes in olive
    oil, drained and finely chopped, but
    reserve 2 tbsp of the oil
freshly ground black pepper

coriander

egg

pumpkin

garlic

flour

ricotta
cheese

sun-dried tomatoes

1 Place the flour, eggs, salt and coriander into a food processor. Pulse until combined.

2 Place the dough on a lightly floured board and knead well for 5 minutes, until smooth. Wrap in plastic wrap and leave to rest in the fridge for 20 minutes.

3 Preheat the oven to 400°F. Place the garlic cloves on a cookie sheet and bake for 10 minutes until softened. Steam the pumpkin for 5–8 minutes until tender and drain well. Peel the garlic cloves and mash into the pumpkin together with the ricotta and drained sun-dried tomatoes. Season with black pepper.

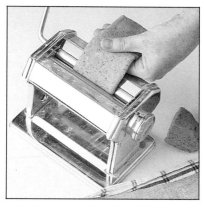

4 Divide the pasta into 4 pieces and flatten slightly. Using a pasta machine, on its thinnest setting, roll out each piece. Leave the sheets of pasta on a clean dish-towel until slightly dried.

5 Using a 3 in crinkle-edged round cutter, stamp out 36 rounds.

6 Top 18 of the rounds with a teaspoonful of mixture, brush the edges with water and place another round of pasta on top. Press firmly around the edges to seal. Bring a large pan of water to a boil, add the ravioli and cook for 3–4 minutes. Drain well and toss into the reserved tomato oil. Serve garnished with coriander sprigs.

Capellini with Arugula, Snow Peas and Pine Nuts

A light but filling pasta dish with the added pepperiness of fresh arugula.

Serves 4

INGREDIENTS
9 oz capellini or angel-hair pasta
8 oz snow peas
6 oz arugula
¼ cup pine nuts, roasted
2 tbsp Parmesan cheese, finely grated (optional)
2 tbsp olive oil (optional)

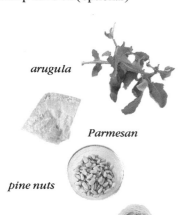

arugula

Parmesan

pine nuts

capellini

snow peas

1 Cook the capellini or angel-hair pasta following the instructions on the side of the package until *al dente*.

2 Meanwhile, carefully top and tail the snow peas.

3 As soon as the pasta is cooked, drop in the arugula and snow peas. Drain immediately.

4 Toss the pasta with the roasted pine nuts, and Parmesan and olive oil if using. Serve at once.

COOK'S TIP
Olive oil and Parmesan are optional as they obviously raise the fat content.

Pasta Bows with Fennel and Walnut Sauce

A scrumptious blend of walnuts and crisp steamed fennel.

Serves 4

INGREDIENTS

½ cup walnuts, shelled and roughly
   chopped
1 garlic clove
1 oz fresh flat-leaf parsley leaves,
   picked from the stems
½ cup ricotta cheese
1 lb pasta bows
1 lb fennel bulbs
chopped walnuts, to garnish

garlic

pasta bows

ricotta

fennel

parsley

walnut halves

chopped walnuts

1 Place the chopped walnuts, garlic and parsley in a food processor. Pulse until roughly chopped. Transfer to a bowl and stir in the ricotta.

2 Cook the pasta following the instructions on the side of the package until *al dente*. Drain well.

3 Slice the fennel thinly and steam for 4–5 minutes until just tender but still crisp.

4 Return the pasta to the pan and add the walnut mixture and the fennel. Toss well and sprinkle with the chopped walnuts. Serve immediately.

Spring Vegetable Stir-fry

A colorful, dazzling medley of fresh and sweet young vegetables.

Serves 4

INGREDIENTS
1 tbsp peanut oil
1 garlic clove, sliced
1 in piece of fresh ginger root, finely
  chopped
4 oz baby carrots
4 oz patty pan squash
4 oz baby corn
4 oz green beans, topped and tailed
4 oz sugar-snap peas, topped and
  tailed
4 oz young asparagus, cut into 3 in
  pieces
8 scallions, trimmed and cut into 2 in
  pieces
4 oz cherry tomatoes

FOR THE DRESSING
juice of 2 limes
1 tbsp honey
1 tbsp soy sauce
1 tsp sesame oil

1 Heat the peanut oil in a wok or large frying pan.

2 Add the garlic and ginger and stir-fry over a high heat for 1 minute.

3 Add the carrots, patty pan squash, baby corn and beans and stir-fry for another 3–4 minutes.

4 Add the sugar-snap peas, asparagus, scallions and cherry tomatoes and stir-fry for a further 1–2 minutes.

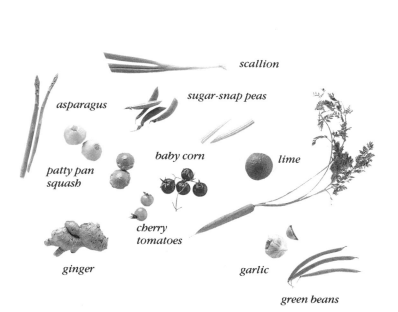

scallion

asparagus

sugar-snap peas

patty pan squash

baby corn

lime

cherry tomatoes

ginger

garlic

green beans

5 Mix the dressing ingredients together and add to the pan.

6 Stir well then cover the pan. Cook for 2–3 minutes more until the vegetables are just tender but still crisp.

COOK'S TIP
Stir-fries take only moments to cook so prepare this dish at the last minute.

Spinach and Potato Galette

Creamy layers of potato, spinach and herbs make a warming supper dish.

Serves 6

INGREDIENTS
2 lb large potatoes
1 lb fresh spinach
2 eggs
14 oz (1¾ cups) low-fat cream
   cheese
1 tbsp grainy mustard
3 tbsp chopped fresh herbs (e.g.
   chives, parsley, chervil or sorrel)
salt and freshly ground black pepper

mustard

parsley

cream cheese

spinach

egg

potatoes

chives

cherry tomatoes

chervil

sorrel

1 Preheat the oven to 350°F. Line a deep 9 in cake pan with parchment paper. Place the potatoes in a large pot and cover with cold water. Bring to a boil and cook for 10 minutes. Drain well and allow to cool slightly before peeling and slicing thinly.

2 Wash the spinach well and place in a large pot with only the water that is clinging to the leaves. Cover and cook, stirring once, until the spinach has just wilted. Drain well in a sieve and squeeze out the excess moisture. Chop finely.

3 Beat the eggs with the cream cheese and mustard then stir in the chopped spinach and fresh herbs.

4 Place a layer of the sliced potatoes in the lined pan, arranging them in concentric circles. Top with a spoonful of the cream cheese mixture and spread out. Continue layering, seasoning with salt and pepper as you go, until all the potatoes and the cream cheese mixture are used up.

5 Cover the pan with a piece of foil and place in a roasting pan.

6 Fill the roasting pan with enough boiling water to come halfway up the sides, and cook in the oven for 45–50 minutes. Turn out onto a plate and serve hot or cold.

COOK'S TIP

Choose firm white or red skinned boiling potatoes for this dish.

Grilled Mixed Peppers with Feta and Green Salsa

Soft, smoky grilled peppers make a lovely combination with the slightly tart salsa.

Serves 4

INGREDIENTS
4 medium peppers in different colors
3 tbsp chopped fresh flat-leaf parsley
3 tbsp chopped fresh dill
3 tbsp chopped fresh mint
½ small red onion, finely chopped
1 tbsp capers, coarsely chopped
¼ cup Greek olives, pitted and sliced
1 fresh green chilli, seeded and finely chopped
4 tbsp pistachios, chopped
5 tbsp extra-virgin olive oil
3 tbsp fresh lime juice
½ cup medium-fat feta cheese, crumbled
1 oz cornichons, finely chopped

olives

feta cheese

green chilli

mint

pistachios

peppers

cornichons

red onion

I Preheat the broiler. Place the whole peppers on a tray and broil until charred and blistered.

2 Place the peppers in a plastic bag and leave to cool.

COOK'S TIP
Feta cheese is quite salty so if preferred, soak in cold water and drain well before using.

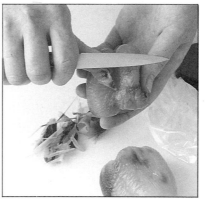

3 Peel, seed and cut the peppers into even strips.

4 Mix all the remaining ingredients together, and stir in the pepper strips.

Beet and Celeriac Gratin

Beautiful ruby-red slices of beets and celeriac make a stunning light accompaniment to any main course dish.

Serves 6

INGREDIENTS
12 oz raw beets
12 oz celeriac
4 thyme sprigs
6 juniper berries, crushed
salt and freshly ground black pepper
½ cup fresh orange juice
½ cup vegetable stock

celeriac

orange juice

juniper berries

beet

thyme

1 Preheat the oven to 375°F. Scrub, peel and slice the beets very finely. Scrub, quarter and peel the celeriac and slice very finely.

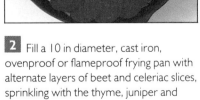

2 Fill a 10 in diameter, cast iron, ovenproof or flameproof frying pan with alternate layers of beet and celeriac slices, sprinkling with the thyme, juniper and seasoning between each layer.

3 Mix the orange juice and stock together and pour over the gratin. Place over a medium heat and bring to a boil. Boil for 2 minutes.

4 Cover with foil and place in the oven for 15–20 minutes. Remove the foil and raise the oven temperature to 400°F. Cook for a further 10 minutes until tender and bubbling.

Eggplant, Roast Garlic and Red Pepper Pâté

This is a simple pâté of smoky baked eggplant, sweet pink peppercorns and red peppers, with more than a hint of garlic!

Serves 4

INGREDIENTS
3 medium eggplants
2 red peppers
5 whole garlic cloves
1½ tsp pink peppercorns in brine, drained and crushed
2 tbsp chopped fresh coriander

eggplant

garlic

coriander

pink peppercorns

red pepper

1 Preheat the oven to 400°F. Arrange the whole eggplants, peppers and garlic cloves on a cookie sheet and place in the oven. After 10 minutes remove the garlic cloves and turn over the eggplants and peppers.

2 Peel the garlic cloves and place in the bowl of a blender.

3 After a further 20 minutes remove the blistered and charred peppers from the oven and place in a paper bag. Leave to cool.

4 After a further 10 minutes remove the eggplants from the oven. Split in half and scoop the flesh into a sieve placed over a bowl. Press the flesh with a spoon to remove the bitter juices.

5 Add the mixture to the garlic in the blender and blend until smooth. Place in a large mixing bowl.

6 Peel and chop the red peppers and stir into the eggplant mixture. Mix in the peppercorns and fresh coriander and serve at once.

Zucchini and Asparagus en Papillote

An impressive dinner party accompaniment, these puffed paper parcels should be broken open at the table by each guest, so that the wonderful aroma can be fully appreciated.

Serves 4

INGREDIENTS
2 medium zucchini
1 medium leek
8 oz young asparagus, trimmed
4 tarragon sprigs
4 whole garlic cloves, unpeeled
salt and freshly ground black pepper
1 egg, beaten

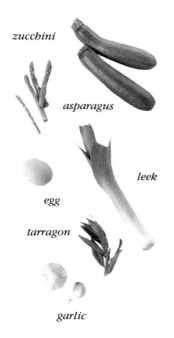

zucchini

asparagus

leek

egg

tarragon

garlic

1 Preheat the oven to 400°F. Using a potato peeler slice the zucchini lengthwise into thin strips.

2 Cut the leek into very fine julienne strips and cut the asparagus evenly into 2 in lengths.

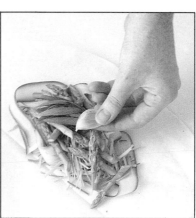

3 Cut out 4 sheets of parchment paper 12 × 15 in in size and fold each in half. Draw a large curve to make a heart shape when unfolded. Cut along the inside of the line and open out.

4 Divide the zucchini, asparagus and leek evenly between each paper heart, positioning the filling on one side of the fold line, and topping each with a sprig of tarragon and an unpeeled garlic clove. Season to taste.

COOK'S TIP

Experiment with other vegetables and herbs such as sugar-snap peas and mint or baby carrots and rosemary. The possibilities are endless.

5 Brush the edges lightly with the beaten egg and fold over.

6 Pleat the edges together so that each parcel is completely sealed. Lay the parcels on a cookie sheet and cook for 10 minutes. Serve immediately.

Broccoli and Chestnut Terrine

Served hot or cold, this versatile terrine is equally suitable for a dinner party as for a picnic.

Serves 4–6

INGREDIENTS
1 lb broccoli, cut into small florets
8 oz cooked chestnuts, roughly chopped
1 cup fresh wholewheat breadcrumbs
4 tbsp low-fat plain yogurt
2 tbsp Parmesan cheese, finely grated
salt, grated nutmeg and freshly ground black pepper
2 eggs, beaten

yogurt

breadcrumbs

broccoli

chestnuts

egg

Parmesan

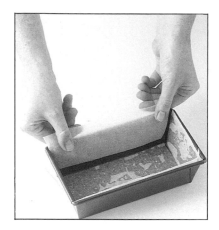

1 Preheat the oven to 350°F. Line a 2 lb loaf pan with a generous layer of parchment paper.

2 Blanch or steam the broccoli for 3–4 minutes until just tender. Drain well. Reserve ¼ of the smallest florets and chop the rest finely.

3 Mix together the chestnuts, breadcrumbs, yogurt and Parmesan, and season to taste.

4 Fold in the chopped broccoli, reserved florets and the beaten eggs.

5 Spoon the broccoli mixture into the prepared pan.

6 Place in a roasting pan and pour in boiling water to come halfway up the sides of the loaf pan. Bake for 20–25 minutes. Remove from the oven and tip out onto a plate or tray. Serve cut into even slices.

Baked Squash

A creamy, sweet and nutty filling makes the perfect topping for tender buttery squash.

Serves 4

INGREDIENTS

2 butternut or acorn squash, 1¼ lb each
1 tbsp olive oil
¾ cup canned corn kernels, drained
½ cup unsweetened chestnut purée
5 tbsp low-fat yogurt
salt and freshly ground black pepper
¼ cup fresh goat cheese
snipped chives, to garnish

yogurt

chestnut purée

corn

butternut squash

goat cheese

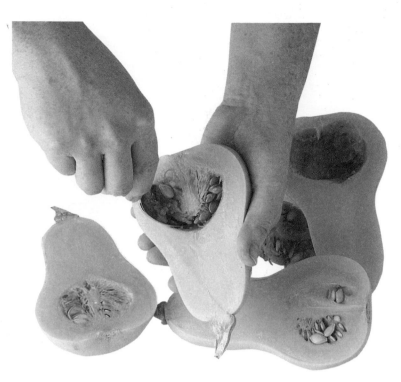

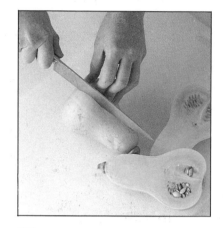

1 Preheat the oven to 350°F. Cut the squash in half lengthwise.

2 Scoop out the seeds with a spoon and discard.

3 Place the squash halves on a cookie sheet and brush the flesh lightly with the oil. Bake in the oven for 30 minutes.

4 Mix together the corn, chestnut purée and yogurt in a bowl. Season to taste.

5 Remove the squash from the oven and divide the chestnut mixture between them, spooning it into the hollows.

COOK'S TIP

Use mozzarella or other mild, soft cheeses in place of goat cheese. The cheese can be omitted entirely for a lower-fat alternative.

6 Top each half with ¼ of the goat cheese and return to the oven for a further 10–15 minutes. Garnish with snipped chives.

Mushroom and Okra Curry with Fresh Mango Relish

This simple but delicious curry with its fresh gingery mango relish is best served with plain basmati rice.

Serves 4

INGREDIENTS
4 garlic cloves, roughly chopped
1 in piece of fresh ginger root, peeled and roughly chopped
1–2 red chillies, seeded and chopped
¾ cup cold water
1 tbsp sunflower oil
1 tsp coriander seeds
1 tsp cumin seeds
1 tsp ground cumin
2 green cardamom pods, seeds removed and ground
pinch of ground turmeric
1 × 14 oz can chopped tomatoes
1 lb mushrooms, halved or quartered if large
8 oz okra, trimmed and cut into ½ in slices
2 tbsp chopped fresh coriander
basmati rice, to serve

FOR THE MANGO RELISH
1 large ripe mango, about 1¼ lb in weight
1 small garlic clove, crushed
1 onion, finely chopped
2 tsp grated fresh ginger root
1 fresh red chilli, seeded and finely chopped
pinch of salt and sugar

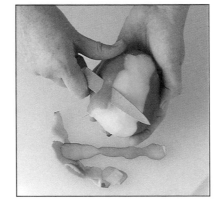

I For the mango relish, peel the mango and cut off the flesh from the pit.

2 In a bowl mash the mango flesh with a fork or pulse in a food processor, and mix in the rest of the relish ingredients. Set to one side.

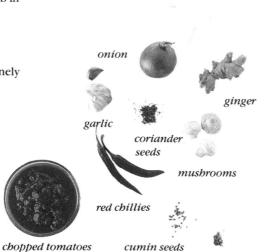

3 Place the garlic, ginger, chilli and 3 tbsp of the water into a blender and blend until smooth.

4 Heat the sunflower oil in a large pan. Add the whole coriander and cumin seeds and allow them to sizzle for a few seconds. Add the ground cumin, ground cardamom and turmeric and cook for 1 minute more.

onion

ginger

garlic

coriander seeds

mushrooms

mango

okra

red chillies

chopped tomatoes

cumin seeds

turmeric

cardamom pods

5 Add the paste from the blender, the tomatoes, remaining water, mushrooms and okra. Stir to mix well and bring to a boil. Reduce the heat, cover, and simmer for 5 minutes.

6 Remove the cover, turn up the heat slightly and cook for another 5–10 minutes until the okra is tender. Stir in the fresh coriander and serve with rice and the mango relish.

Potato Gnocchi with Hazelnut Sauce

These delicate potato dumplings are dressed with a creamy hazelnut sauce.

Serves 4

INGREDIENTS
1 ½ lb large potatoes
1 cup plain flour

FOR THE HAZELNUT SAUCE
½ cup skinned, roasted hazelnuts
1 garlic clove, roughly chopped
½ tsp grated lemon rind
½ tsp lemon juice
2 tbsp sunflower oil
scant ¾ cup low-fat ricotta cheese
salt and freshly ground black pepper

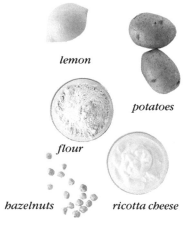

lemon

potatoes

flour

hazelnuts

ricotta cheese

garlic

1 Place ⅓ cup of the hazelnuts in a blender with the garlic, grated lemon rind and juice. Blend until coarsely chopped. Gradually add the oil and blend until smooth. Spoon into a bowl and mix in the ricotta cheese. Season to taste.

2 Place the potatoes in a pan of cold water. Bring to the boil and cook for 20–25 minutes. Drain well in a colander.

When cool, peel and purée the potatoes while still warm by passing them through a food mill into a bowl.

3 Add the flour a little at a time (you may not need all the flour as potatoes vary in texture). Stop adding flour when the mixture is smooth and slightly sticky. Add salt to taste.

4 Roll out the mixture onto a floured board, into a long sausage about ½ in in diameter. Cut into ¾ in lengths.

5 Take 1 piece at a time and press it on to a floured fork. Roll each piece slightly while pressing it along the prongs and off the fork. Flip onto a floured plate or tray. Continue with the rest of the mixture.

COOK'S TIP

A light touch is the key to making soft gnocchi, so handle the dough as little as possible to prevent the mixture from becoming tough.

6 Bring a large pan of water to a boil and drop in 20–25 pieces at a time. They will rise to the surface very quickly. Let them cook for 10–15 seconds more, then lift them out with a slotted spoon. Drop into a dish and keep warm. Continue with the rest of the gnocchi. To heat the sauce, place in a heatproof bowl over a pot of simmering water and heat gently, being careful not to let the sauce curdle. Pour the sauce over the gnocchi. Roughly chop the remaining hazelnuts and scatter over the sauce.

Zucchini and Walnut Loaf

Cardamom seeds impart their distinctive aroma to this loaf. Serve spread with ricotta and honey for a delicious snack.

Makes 1 loaf

INGREDIENTS

3 eggs
⅓ cup light brown sugar, firmly
   packed
½ cup sunflower oil
2 cups wholewheat flour
1 tsp baking powder
1 tsp baking soda
1 tsp ground cinnamon
¾ tsp ground allspice
½ tbsp green cardamoms, seeds
   removed and crushed
5 oz zucchini, coarsely grated
½ cup walnuts, chopped
¼ cup sunflower seeds

zucchini

walnuts

egg

sunflower oil

brown sugar

wholewheat flour

sunflower seeds

cardamom pods

1 Preheat the oven to 350°F. Line the base and sides of a 2 lb loaf pan with parchment paper.

2 Beat the eggs and sugar together and gradually add the oil.

3 Sift the flour into a bowl together with the baking powder, baking soda, cinnamon and allspice.

4 Mix into the egg mixture with the rest of the ingredients, reserving 1 tbsp of the sunflower seeds for the top.

5 Spoon into the loaf tin, level off the top, and sprinkle with the reserved sunflower seeds.

6 Bake for 1 hour or until a skewer inserted in the center comes out clean. Leave to cool slightly before turning out onto a wire rack to cool completely.

Red Pepper and Watercress Filo Parcels

Peppery watercress combines well with sweet red pepper in these crisp little parcels.

Makes 8

INGREDIENTS
3 red peppers
6 oz watercress
1 cup ricotta cheese
¼ cup blanched almonds, toasted
    and chopped
salt and freshly ground black pepper
8 sheets of filo pastry
2 tbsp olive oil

ricotta

red pepper

watercress

almonds

filo pastry

1 Preheat the oven to 375°F. Place the peppers under a hot broiler until blistered and charred. Place in a paper bag. When cool enough to handle peel, seed and pat dry on kitchen paper.

2 Place the peppers and watercress in a food processor and pulse until coarsely chopped. Spoon into a bowl.

3 Mix in the ricotta and almonds, and season to taste.

4 Working with 1 sheet of filo pastry at a time, cut out 2 × 7 in and 2 × 2 in squares from each sheet. Brush 1 large square with a little olive oil and place a second large square at an angle of 90 degrees to form a star shape.

5 Place 1 of the small squares in the center of the star shape, brush lightly with oil and top with a second small square.

6 Top with ⅛ of the red pepper mixture. Bring the edges together to form a purse shape and twist to seal. Place on a lightly greased cookie sheet and cook for 25–30 minutes until golden.

Sage Soda Bread

This wonderful loaf, quite unlike bread made with yeast, has a velvety texture and a powerful sage aroma.

Makes 1 loaf

INGREDIENTS
2 cups wholewheat flour
1 cup flour
½ tsp salt
1 tsp baking soda
2 tbsp shredded fresh sage or 2 tsp
  dried sage, crumbled
1¼–1¾ cups buttermilk

white flour

wholewheat flour

sage

buttermilk

1 Preheat the oven to 425°F. Sift the dry ingredients into a bowl.

2 Stir in the sage and add enough buttermilk to make a soft dough.

COOK'S TIP

As an alternative to the sage, try using finely chopped rosemary or thyme.

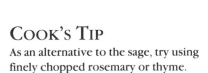

3 Shape the dough into a round loaf and place on a lightly oiled cookie sheet.

4 Cut a deep cross in the top. Bake in the oven for 40 minutes until the loaf is well risen and sounds hollow when tapped on the bottom. Leave to cool on a wire rack.

Mini Pizzas

For a quick supper dish try these delicious little pizzas made with fresh and sun-dried tomatoes.

Makes 4

INGREDIENTS

1 × 5 oz package pizza mix
8 halves sun-dried tomatoes in olive
  oil, drained
½ cup black olives, pitted
8 oz ripe tomatoes, sliced
¼ cup goat cheese
2 tbsp fresh basil leaves

basil

tomatoes

*sun-dried
tomatoes*

black olives

goat cheese

1 Preheat the oven to 400°F. Make up the pizza base following the instructions on the side of the package.

2 Divide the dough into 4 and roll each piece out to a 5 in disc. Place on a lightly oiled cookie sheet.

3 Place the sun-dried tomatoes and olives in a blender or food processor and blend until smooth. Spread the mixture evenly over the pizza bases.

4 Top with the tomato slices and crumble over the goat cheese. Bake for 10–15 minutes. Sprinkle with the fresh basil and serve.

Parsnip and Pecan Cheese Puffs with Watercress and Arugula Sauce

These scrumptious nutty puffs conceal a surprisingly sweet parsnip center.

Makes 18

INGREDIENTS
½ cup butter
1¼ cups water
¾ cup plain flour
½ cup wholewheat flour
3 eggs, beaten
1 oz Cheddar cheese, grated
pinch of cayenne pepper or paprika
⅓ cup pecans, chopped
1 medium parsnip, cut into
    ¾ in pieces
1 tbsp skim milk
2 tsp sesame seeds

FOR THE SAUCE
5 oz watercress, trimmed
5 oz arugula, trimmed
¾ cup low-fat yogurt
salt, grated nutmeg and freshly ground
    black pepper
watercress sprigs, to garnish

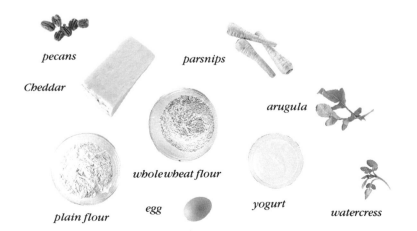

pecans

Cheddar

parsnips

arugula

wholewheat flour

plain flour

egg

yogurt

watercress

1 Preheat the oven to 400°F. Place the butter and water in a pot. Bring to a boil and add all the flour at once. Beat vigorously until the mixture leaves the sides of the pan and forms a ball. Remove from heat and allow the mixture to cool slightly. Beat in the eggs a little at a time until the mixture is shiny and soft enough to fall gently from a spoon.

2 Beat in the Cheddar, cayenne pepper or paprika and the chopped pecans.

3 Lightly grease a cookie sheet and drop onto it 18 heaped tablespoons of the mixture. Place a piece of parsnip on each and top with another heaped tablespoon of the mixture.

4 Brush the puffs with a little milk and sprinkle with sesame seeds. Bake in the oven for 25–30 minutes until golden.

5 Meanwhile make the sauce. Bring a pan of water to a boil and blanch the watercress and arugula for 2–3 minutes. Drain and immediately refresh in cold water. Drain well and chop.

6 Purée the watercress and arugula in a blender or food processor with the yogurt until smooth. Season to taste with salt, nutmeg and freshly ground black pepper. To reheat, place the sauce in a bowl over a gently simmering pot of hot water and heat gently, taking care not to let the sauce curdle. Garnish with watercress.

Tomato Breadsticks

Once you've tried this simple recipe you'll never buy manufactured breadsticks again. Serve with aperitifs, with a dip or with cheese to end a meal.

Makes 16

INGREDIENTS
2 cups plain flour
½ tsp salt
½ tbsp easy-blend dry yeast
1 tsp honey
1 tsp olive oil
⅔ cup warm water
6 halves sun-dried tomatoes in olive
   oil, drained and chopped
1 tbsp skim milk
2 tsp poppy seeds

plain flour

sun-dried tomatoes

honey

yeast

poppy seeds

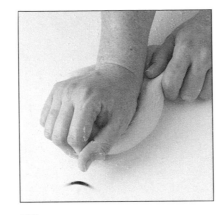

1 Place the flour. salt and yeast in a food processor. Add the honey and olive oil and, with the machine running, gradually pour in the water (you may not need it all as flours vary). Stop adding water as soon as the dough starts to cling together. Process for 1 minute more.

2 Turn out the dough onto a floured board and knead for 3–4 minutes until springy and smooth. Knead in the chopped sun-dried tomatoes. Form into a ball and place in a lightly oiled bowl. Leave to rise for 5 minutes.

3 Preheat the oven to 300°F. Divide the dough into 16 equal pieces and roll each piece into a 11 in × ½ in long stick. Place on a lightly oiled cookie sheet and leave to rise in a warm place for 15 minutes.

4 Brush the sticks with milk and sprinkle with poppy seeds. Bake for 30 minutes. Leave to cool on a wire rack.

Oatmeal Tartlets with Minted Hummus

Serve these wholesome little tartlets with a crisp salad of Boston lettuce.

Serves 6

INGREDIENTS
1½ cups medium oatmeal
½ tsp baking soda
1 tsp salt
2 tbsp butter
1 egg yolk
2 tbsp skim milk
1 × 14 oz can chick-peas, rinsed and
    drained
juice of 1–2 lemons
1½ cups ricotta cheese
4 tbsp tahini
freshly ground black pepper
3 tbsp chopped fresh mint
2 tbsp pumpkin seeds
paprika, for dusting

pumpkin seeds

tahini

ricotta cheese

chick-peas

oatmeal

mint

lemon

1 Preheat the oven to 325°F. Mix together the oatmeal, baking soda and salt in a large bowl. Rub in the butter until the mixture resembles fine breadcrumbs. Stir in the egg yolk and add the milk if the mixture seems too dry.

2 Press into 3½ in tartlet pans. Bake for 25–30 minutes. Allow to cool.

3 Purée the chick-peas, the juice of 1 lemon, ricotta cheese and tahini in a food processor until smooth. Spoon into a bowl and season with black pepper and more lemon juice to taste. Stir in the chopped mint. Divide between the tartlet moulds, sprinkle with pumpkin seeds and dust with paprika.

Saffron Focaccia

A dazzling yellow bread that is light in texture and distinctive in flavor.

Makes 1 loaf

INGREDIENTS
pinch of saffron threads
⅔ cup boiling water
2 cups flour
½ tsp salt
1 tsp easy-blend dry yeast
1 tbsp olive oil

FOR THE TOPPING
2 garlic cloves, sliced
1 red onion, cut into thin wedges
rosemary sprigs
12 black olives, pitted and coarsely
    chopped
1 tbsp olive oil

flour

garlic

rosemary

red onion

olives

saffron

yeast

1 Place the saffron in a heatproof cup and pour on the boiling water. Leave to stand and infuse until lukewarm.

2 Place the flour, salt, yeast and olive oil in a food processor. Turn on and gradually add the saffron and its liquid. Process until the dough forms into a ball.

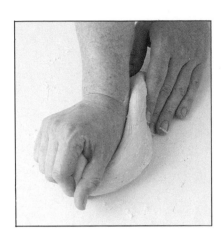

3 Turn onto a floured board and knead for 10–15 minutes. Place in a bowl, cover and leave to rise for 30–40 minutes until doubled in size.

4 Punch down the risen dough on a lightly floured surface and roll out into an oval shape, ½ in thick. Place on a lightly greased cookie sheet and leave to rise for 20–30 minutes.

5 Preheat the oven to 400°F. Press small indentations all over the surface of the focaccia with your fingers.

6 Cover with the topping ingredients, brush lightly with olive oil, and bake for 25 minutes or until the loaf sounds hollow when tapped on the bottom. Leave to cool on a wire rack.

INDEX